RISED BY PIMPS, PLAYERS AND MURDERERS.

By

Timothy D. Mitchell.

COPYRIGHT © 2019. ALL RIGHTS RESERVED.

No part of this publication may be reproduced, distributed, or transmitted in any form or by any means, including photocopying, recording, or other electronic or mechanical methods, or by any information storage and retrieval system without the prior written permission of the publisher, except in the case of very brief quotations embodied in critical reviews and certain other noncommercial uses permitted by copyright law.

Table of Contents
Introduction

CHAPTER ONE

THE MIND

CHAPTER TWO

CHANGE YOUR THINKING, CHANGE YOUR LIFE

CHAPTER THREE

THE HAPPY STATE

CHAPTER FOUR

PRACTICE MIND CONTROL

CHAPTER FIVE

THE POWER OF REFLECTION

CHAPTER SIX

SECRETS AND SURPRISES

Introduction

My name is Timothy D. Mitchell. I was born in the mid 60's in St. Louis Mo. Home of the Gateway Arch.

I now resided in the Motor City Detroit Mi. I don't remember the day I was born. But I can remember some events and situations from age of 3 years old. I do remember a awful lot from the age of 5. I remember starting kindergarten at Cook Elementary.

If you look closely. You'll see the steps that lead down to the kindergarten class rooms and play-ground. Believe it or not I skip class on them steps. I decided not to go into class and just sit on the steps till class was over. I got a good butt whooping for that.

Two of my favorite songs back the 70's where Never can say goodbye by the Jackson 5 and Ain't no sunshine by Bill Withers. But my overall favorite group of the 70's and still to this day is the Isley Brothers.

I came to love their music so much, till my funeral song is Voyage to Atlantis. They are my personal favorite group from that time. Can't forget Earth Wind & Fire, Al Green, Bobby Womack, The Emotions, Berry White,The Temptations, Stevie Wonder, Marvin Gaye, C.C.R, Paul McCartney,Chicago,Led Zeppelin,Queen David Bowie etc. I can go on forever. The music in the 70's was just sooooooooooo awesome.

Urban Dictionary meaning of a Pimp: A ni**ga that keeps his hoe's in check.

PIMP:
P-Person
I-Into
M-Marketing
P-Prostitutes

Also in the 70's, A Pimp was the thing to be. Pimp's had money, homes,cars,clothes and hoe's. This is known as Pimp-economy. The movie most popular for glorifying pimping and was made in the 70's is The Mack.

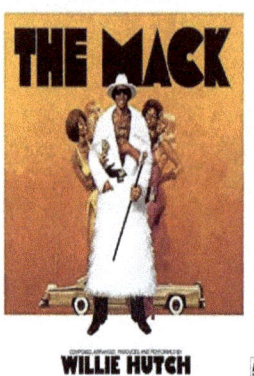

This movie showed how a person can have **Mind Control** over another person(women). How else can you persuade a women to sell her body for you and she receives little to nothing in return. If she didn't cooperate or came up short with money, they where beaten.

Talking about mind control. I remember as a kid. This guy was going to give me a ride home. But I had to wait till he got off the phone, before we could leave. He was talking talking to some lady on the phone. She made him mad about something. The last thing he said before he hung up was; have your ass there so I can beat your ass. He said to me lets go, but we have to make a stop so I can whoop this bitch ass. Sure enough she was waiting in the car where he said to be at. We pulled up besides her. He said to me wait here, I'll be back.

He got in the car with her and just started punching and slapping this lady for a least 3 or 4 minutes. I couldn't believe what I was seeing. When he got back in the car with me, he said sometimes you gotta let these hoe's know who's the boss. He had so much mind control over this woman till he could tell her where to be for her whooping. **That's Powerful.**

Don't get PIMPED

Urban Dictionary meaning of a Player:

Usually a male or female who makes you feel special. They make you feel like you are the only one in their life, when really you are just one in 100. They flirt with other people, not just you. They talk to you all day, then the next day they ignore you. They send you mixed messages and you're not sure whether he or she likes you or not. You can't keep your mind off them.

Players can be male or female. They are usually slick, dress nicely and are very charming.

They prey on people socially usually looking for sex or money. They have a way of befriending people and making them feel important, before they use them to their own ends.

In my young and impressionable life. I seen and was taught how to be a player, way way way before the 1997 film; How To Be A Player was even thought of.

This film left out so many facts on becoming a player, till it was hard for me to watch. One great thing this movie did do. Was have the ultimate player/pimp; Max Julien from the movie The Mack appear in the movie.

Bottom line to be a Player. You have to know how to keep things **Hidden.** You could say I got free tuition at Player Academy. I was thinking of a story I can tell how a player operates. There are so many, till I don't know where to start.

Here's something. Still living in St. Louis before the age of 11. I always wanted to spend time with my babysitter. I taught she was the most beautiful thing on this earth. But I was too young for her. I was around her a lot. So I was able to see a lot things. She had multiple boyfriends. I knew them but they didn't know each other. Now in those days, there was no caller ID. So certain boyfriends had to ring the phone a certain way, at a certain time. She told each boyfriend a story why they had to call that way. But the real reason was because she may have one of he boyfriends at the house. They all knew not to come over without asking first. If they did come without calling, she wouldn't let them in or answer the door. Well like I said, I was around her a lot so I even knew the rings for each boyfriend.

Me being jealous that I can't be her boyfriend. She had one of her boyfriends at the house. They were sitting on the couch watching T.V. The phone ringed, I seen what time it was and knew it was a boyfriend calling. I answer the phone before it could finish it's ringed pattern. It was one of her other boyfriends. He ask to speak to her, I gave her the phone while she was sitting on the couch next to the boyfriend at the house. I said to myself she gonna get it now. **WRONG!!!!!!!!!!**

She talk to him on the phone all cool, calm and collective. Didn't miss a beat. They talked almost an hour. She was so skilled at what to say and not to say till the boyfriend sitting next to her didn't think she was talking to another guy. Even when she hung up with him, the boyfriend sitting next to her ask who was she talking to. She said and old friend she hadn't heard from in a while. He just said OK.

After he left. She said to me; **Don't you know I'm a player?** Because I did that, she said I couldn't come over for a month. That killed me. After the month was up. I knew to keep my mouth shut and don't play any games. I went back to St. Louis from michigan for a visit to find-out she still is a **PLAYER.**

Urban Dictionary meaning of a Murderer: A person who kills other people.

The 70's is one of the worst decades for murders. I can remember just about everytime looking at the news, seeing someone been shot or murdered. I can't begin to tell you how many guns I've seen and even played with a gun. I was told by my baby-sitter when I was 3, I her mother's boyfriends gun in the drawer. I put it to his head when he was bent over in the refrigerator. I use to play with my step-dad when he would leave for work. By the grace of God I didn't shoot or kill myself.

I won't go into detail. But I do know and I'm related to people who have killed. They've all have done prison time, still incarcerated.

Growing up as a kid then into my teenage years. I was around these types of people (Pimp,Players & Murderers) on a daily bassis. My family had weekend parties starting from friday evening to sunday evening. I can remember having these parties since I was 5 years old. They go further than that. Last I heard these parties still carry on to this day. I was the one who played the records for them. Or you can say I was the DJ. So when I hear songs from the 70's, it brings back so many memories of places, times, stories and people.

What I most remember is; when these people would get drunk. They always needed someone to listen to them as they got things off their chest. Well guess who had to listen to them? You guessed it. Some of the stories I listen to, a kid shouldn't be hearing. Not only would I get told stories. These adults always felt the need to teach me about life.

As a child you didn't really care to listen to grown folks unless, they were talking about doing something for you. I had to listen to these stories and teachings every weekend for some years. Not only was it men teaching me about life it was women also. I use to get so sick and tired of hearing them tell me how to live, till I would say to myself; I wish they would shut-up, please pass out or you don't know what you're talking about.

Would you believe the people I thought of as; old buzzers,drunks, bums and the ones who were the Pimp, Players & Murderers. These people really did know what they were talking about. As I got older into high school on to living as an adult. I started being in the exact situations they talked about. By them talking to me so much about situations. I knew exactly how to handle the situations. These people gave me so much knowledge, till there wasn't many situations I couldn't handle.

When I started to look back on each one of these people. None finish High School, none went to trade school, none went to college, most couldn't read, write or spell. Most grew-up in the segregated south during Jim Grow Laws. I realized these people knew what they wanted. Then figured ways to get it. Whether legal or illegal. It just goes to show that we all have the most deadlest weapon on earth. That weapon is the **MIND.**

I remember something a guy told me who called himself a pimp, a player and someone who has shot at people. He said; Let explain how a Pimp, Player and a murderer operate. He said;

A **Pimp** has mind control over a woman. How else can a woman sell her body and get very little in return, while the pimp is living this great life from her selling her body. To keep her selling her body. The pimp has instilled FEAR in her to the point she is afraid to leave him.

A **PLAYER** is someone who can keep things and situations hidden from another person. This is someone who has many women at one time, in which one doesn't know about the other. The same for women who have many men. And can talk their way out of any situation.

A **MURDERER** is a person who surprises there victim. You can't just tell a person I'm going to kill you on a certain day. That person will be able to do what it takes to prevent he or she from being murdered. So you have to come out no-where to kill them.

This particular person who told me this was a close family friend so I was around him a lot. In which I learned a awful lot from him. That's where I get the saying; I was raised by **PIMP, PLAYERS, MURDERERS.**

When you think about it. A Pimp, A Player, A Murderer. These people are seen in a negative way. This is true, you shouldn't won't to be associated with these types of people. But in actuality we associated with these types of people every day.

Think about it.
A Pimp has mind control over his flock of women. He controls them by fear. They are in fear of the consequences, if they don't have the money, come up short and think about leaving their pimp. So the woman feel trap with no-way out of the situation.

How many of us have seen or heard this saying? This is so true. We have mortgages, car payments, utilities bills and many other reoccurring bills. If we don't pay them, we are in fear of loosing everything we own, having our utilities shut off and be homeless. Wouldn't you say the mortgage companies, banks and utilitie companies are pimping us out just like a prostitute.

These necessities are needed to live. You can lessen the amount of control they have over your life. We don't need someone else to live or to feel of value. It's not about how others feel about us, it's about how we feel about ourselves. Just like a Pimp. People will play games with your mind, having you think you need them when they really need you. Their way of putting fear in you is by laying a gult trip on you. If you don't do a certain thing for them, loan them money or bettering your life where you will not need them in you life anymore. These are the things we can control.

Don't fall for this trap. You deserve to be happy. Remember you come first in any situation. You only got one life to live. So live a full and happy life. Control the Pimps in your life, don't let them control your life. When you gain control of your mind. No one can control you.

Avoid people who:
1. Mess with your head.
2. Intentionally and repeatedly do and say that they know upset you.
3. Expect you to prioritize them but refuse to prioritize you.
4. Can't and won't apologise sincerely.
5. Act like the victim when confronted with their abusive behavior.

A **Player** is very good at keeping people, situations and things hidden. There is not much if anything a person can pin on them. I gave one example of this in the story about my babysitter. A popular saying back in the day was; **You Got Played.**

This was said when a person expected a peron or something to be a certain way, only to find out it's not that way at all. You can sign up for a program or service expecting to pay one price, only to have hidden fee's that was unknown to the customer or was written where it couldn't be seen first hand by the customer's. People really feel played when it comes to voting. Political figures say they're going to do or change someting once in office. Only to do hardy if any of the things they promise while running for office.

But mostly in life. People will try to play you or play games with your mind. This is something that is dealth with eveyday.

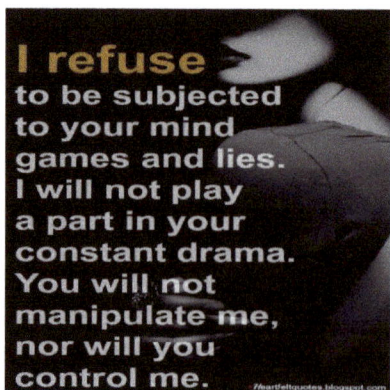

Remember players keep things hidden. If you feel someone is trying or is playing you. Just sit back and wait. A persons true intentions will always show in time. Learn to say no when someone is always asking you for something and don't give back to you in return. Never take a person at their word, unless you've known them a awful long time. Even then you still should look out to see if you're being **PLAYED...**

A **MURDERER** is someone who takes another persons life. This is usually done by surprise. If a person knew another person was planning to kill him, he or she would do whatever it takes to avoid being killed.

A **MURDERER** is not always somebody who kills with a weapon, such has a knife or gun. Actually the most deadlest weapons on earth is the mind and tongue.

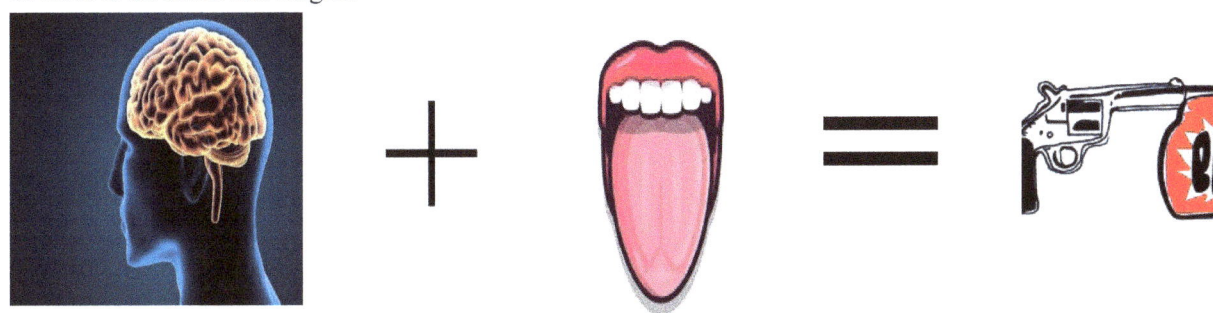

When the mind is added to the tongue it makes the mouth go **BANG...**

What comes out the mouth or gun so to speak is up to you. When you think negative thoughts, then speak them about yourself. You're committing sucide. Which will kill your life. No matter how bad your life may seem. If you are bleessed to see another day. That means there's hope for you. Try to always speak positively on every part of your life. Even when it's hard to do.

Don't be around people who are negative on themselves and you. Those types of people will only bring you down and make you dead to the world. Basically killing you. I myself have been around these types of people. They aways made me feel less than everybody else or achieve greatness. These where people close to me with their way of thinking, and forcing their beliefs on me. Which made me feel I had nothing to live for.

When I started reading self-help books and believing in my higher-power. I was able to to break free from those negative people words of death.

If I can do it. You can also. All you have to do is believe. I remember not to long ago, I was in a bad situation. With no place to go, no job, no where to turn for help. Totally unwanted, burned a lot of bridges, people letting me know what a looser I am. I was dead to the world so to speak. The one thing I kept saying to myself was; **next year at this time I want be in this situation.** All I could do was focus on the future and working toward it.

Due to me not giving up and people murdering me with their mouth. I gain more than I lost. People stopped looking down me, in fact they tired to say I acted like I was better than them. I was like WOW!!!! these are the same people putting me down a few mouths earlier. Not only did I get a job I ended up doing 4 jobs for 3 years. As you can see. When I changed my focus and not let people murder me with their mouth. I was able to do get things with my life. Such as written 4 books.

You can be a murderer and surprise people with the way you're living your life and having fun living it. There's a old saying that comes to my mind it says: **HE/SHE MURDERED IT!!!!!!!!!!!!!!!!!**

This is what you want said about your life, while you're alive and at the end of your life.

It is my hope and dream, that everyone reading this book. Will become a PIMP, PLAYER & MURDERER but in a positive way of life. Thank you for your support.

CHAPTER ONE

THE MIND

Creating a healthy mind is a daily discipline that you should master, just like creating a healthy body. However, one mistake people make is to separate the health of the mind from that of the body. When it comes to good health, people tend to focus only on the body below the neck, but that is wrong, the brain is the organ that keeps the other parts of the body functioning. Mental health, emotional health and physical health are all interwoven.

You brain depends on the physical nutrition it gets from your body to function well and when your brain is healthy, your body is strong as well, enabling you to reduce stress levels, increase energy levels and improve the sharpness of your mind.

Having a healthy mind means that you are in control of your thoughts and determine the direction your mind travels per time. Before new research in neuroscience was done, it was believed that once an adult stops growing, his brain stopped growing as well but this has been proved to be untrue by advances in neuroscience. Neuroplasticity is the ability of the brain to grow and change form over the course of a human's life.

Meditation is a great way to train the mind to focus. When you meditate or perform yoga, you practice how to tune off noise, distractions and other external influences and tune in and focus on your inner self. Meditation helps you connect with your inner self and reach a place of peace and tranquility between the body and the soul. It helps to relieve stress and improve the quality of sleep. It is believed that all the divine powers that a human has lies in his heart and meditation is the only way through which one can get really deep into the heart to unlock these powers.

As a first time practitioner of meditation, you may find that you mind wanders as to try to focus on one thought or an object, but do not fight it, let it happen. Meditation should not be forced. As you let your mind and body calms down, your mind will return to the object it desires to focus on and with time, it will enter into a phase of deep concentration. Meditation will make you calmer and enable you perform your tasks with a serenity that is infectious.

Meditation also helps to control anger and cultivate good habits such as being disciplined and supportive of other people. When you meditate regularly, you develop the ability to be mindful and to live in the moment. This will help you reach the highest point of consciousness and help you learn more about yourself; that is self-awareness and I shall delve more into it in subsequent chapters.

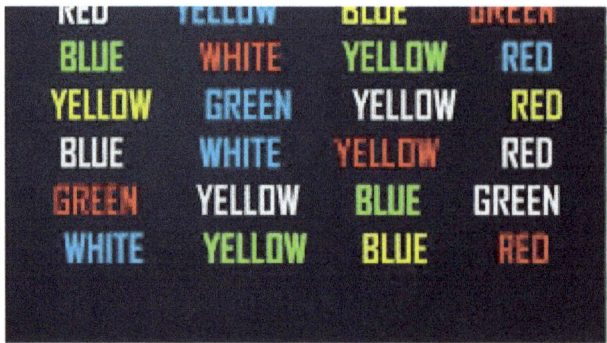

Brain games are also a great way to gain control of the mind. These games help to keep the brain sharp and prevent debilitating brain diseases like Alzheimers, Dementia etc.

There are also sleep programs that have to been connected to phones through apps and which help to track the sleep pattern of a person suffering from insomnia, find out what the causal factors of insomnia may be and make recommendations of remedies for the situation.

The best mind control techniques are the ones that make a difference in how you can practice mind control every day and take control of your life again.

Creative visualization uses emotional intelligence to make visualization of your desired destination or state effective. Creative visualization changes the vibration of what you attract and causes only what you attract to come to you. Creative visualization works in pretty much the same way as the Law of Attraction.

Imagine holding a guitar in your hand and plucking just one string in it. The plucked string will hit the other strings and resonate with them. Creative visualization takes a little more effort and mind –training skills than any other mind control.

A must read for creative visualization..

CHAPTER TWO

CHANGE YOUR THINKING, CHANGE YOUR LIFE

It is certain that not everyone will like you. In fact, you may have more enemies than you can manage but the good news is that you can win them over and turn them to friends if you take the time to do the work required. I have not seen a human who does not respond to love when it is shown to him. True, there are a few people who are natural sadists but I want to believe that at a point, these people needed someone to believe in them and make them feel special but there was no one to do it and that was why they turned out the way they did.

There are very simple things you can do as a person to draw your enemies close and turn them into friends and I am going to be sharing a few of them in this chapter but first, let's start with you and your own attitude to yourself. Who do you think you are? What perception do you have about your person? These are very important questions you should ask yourself because your perception of your own person shines through to others to see, whether you like it or not.

If you think that you are an awesome individual to be with, it exudes from within you and will show automatically in the way you treat others and vice versa when the reverse is the case. You have it in you to be all that you desire to be. Many people believe that some have the ability to interact well even when they are stressed out while others do not because the problems they face and the situations that they find themselves in always determine how they turn out but I believe this is not always true.

I believe that you can all learn to be resilient, and your ability to bounce back from difficult conditions is not based on your genes or even your life experiences, you have it in you already, it is left to you to bring it out of you.

The most powerful people are those who rise up to a challenge and face it with courage and the ability to inspire others to follow them to do things that they ordinarily would not do.

Every improvement you can make in your life stems from changing your beliefs about yourself, your abilities and your possibilities. Your personal growth comes from changing your thinking about what you can do and about what is possible for you. Napoleon Hill said, **"Whatever the mind of man can conceive and believe, it can achieve."**

What you think about your life is what you become. If you think it can be done, then it will be but if you think it isn't possible, then you will not be able to achieve it. Perhaps the greatest breakthrough in this century in the area of human potential was the discovery of self-concept. Everything you do or achieve in your life, every action or thought that you have is controlled and determined by your self-concept. Your self-concept is the way you perceive yourself and it determines your effectiveness and level of performance in all that you do.

Your self-concept is the basic operating system of your mental computer. It is a sum total of all your beliefs, attitudes, feelings an opinions about yourself and your world and that is why you always operate in a manner that is consistent with your self-concept, whether positive or negative.

As you do this, you grow your mind and your capacity to be mindful. The more mindful you are, the better you will be at using your mind well to bring others to your side of perception.

Strive To Understand More Than To Be Understood

Carl Rogers, the eminent psychologist in his book, 'On Becoming a Person' wrote:

I have found it of enormous value that I can permit myself to understand the other person. Now, that may seem strange to you – is it necessary to permit oneself to understand another? I think it is. Our first reaction to most of the statements that we hear from other people is an evaluation or judgment, rather than an understanding of it. When someone expresses some feeling, attitude or belief, our tendency is almost immediately to believe to feel, 'that's right,' or 'that's stupid,' 'that's unrealistic,' 'that's absurd,' 'that's incorrect,' 'that's not good.' Very rarely do we permit ourselves to understand precisely what the meaning of the statement is to the other person."

If you strive to understand the viewpoint of another person, even if you disagree with him, he would see your view point and accept the corrections that you make to him.

Be Optimistic

Attitude is very important and an optimistic attitude is key as well. The act of relating with people in this manner is not always as easy as it sounds. When you are optimistic and confident and you appear so to people, more often than not, it will rub off on them as well. You will scale heights and go beyond yourself to do great things and they will copy you.

However, not all of us are born optimists, it is a quality that can be learned. Learned optimism is the habit of attributing a person's failures to things that occurred to him temporarily. An optimistic learner is one who sees anything that happens to him as an opportunity to learn and grow.

An optimistic learner has also been found to be better academically, in athletics, in relating with people etc. He has better coping skills, less likelihood of succumbing to sadness and depression and has better physical health. It has now been found out that people can be taught how to be more optimistic and resilient than they were before.

How to Be Optimistic When the World Around You Isn't. By:Amy Morin

Sometimes, it's hard to be happy when you think about what's going on in the world. It's harder still when the people around you constantly complain about all those things that are happening.

That doesn't mean that you have to join ranks with the pessimists, though. In fact, it means it's more important than ever to look on the bright side as much as possible.

Benefits of Being Optimistic
Choosing to be optimistic offers surprising benefits. A study from the University of Pittsburgh concluded that women who had an optimistic outlook had a 30 percent lower risk of heart disease. A University of Michigan study linked optimism to a lower risk of stroke. Additionally, research published in the Canadian Medical Association Journal found that optimists are less likely to experience disabilities as they get older and end up living longer than pessimists.

Optimism Is a Choice
If you think you're a natural-born pessimist and there's no way you can turn your mindset around, think again—research published in the Journal of Behavior Therapy and Experimental Psychiatry compared two groups of people to test their thinking patterns.

The first group completed a 5-minute exercise that involved thinking positive thoughts about their future, while the second group just went about their daily lives without making effort to think optimistically.

The first group significantly increased their optimism over the two-week period, with many of them feeling more optimistic after just one day. If you want to become a more optimistic person—despite the negativity surrounding you—then you can take measures to think positively and spread that optimistic outlook to those around you.

Decide to Be Optimistic

You have choices in your life. You can spend the day cleaning or spend the day reading. You can go out to dinner or cook at home. You can have coffee with that long-lost friend or you can blow them off. And, finally, you can decide to be positive or you can just go on living like you are. Being an optimistic person in a negative world begins with the decision to be positive and choosing to live that life every single day.

Avoid Positive Energy Vampires.

You might refer to them as "whiners" or even "toxic," but however you refer to them, pessimists suck the positive energy out of the room. These people think the world revolves around them, and they often lack any sense of empathy for others.

It's important to establish healthy boundaries with people who chronically choose to stay stuck in their own misery. That may mean having to say things to a friend like, "I notice every time I offer you an idea about how you could make your situation better, you insist nothing will work. I am not sure I'm able to help.

It may also mean distancing yourself a bit from a relative who insists on sharing his latest predictions about the end of the world.

Limit your media intake as well.

Watching too many tragic stories on the news or consuming too much political news on social media can decrease your ability to maintain a "glass half full" outlook.

Recognize Your Negative Thoughts.

It's OK to acknowledge that bad things might happen. After all, ignoring reality isn't helpful.
In fact, being realistic could be the key to doing your best. If you're excessively positive about an upcoming interview, you might not spend any time preparing because you're confident you'll land the job. If however, you have an exaggeratedly negative outlook, you might sabotage your chances of getting hired.

Thinking, "No one will ever hire me," will cause you to look and feel defeated when you walk into the interview room. Your lack of confidence may be the reason you don't get hired.

A healthy outlook would be to remind yourself that all you can do is your best and you'll be OK, regardless of the outcome.

Being optimistic helps you believe that brighter opportunities are on the horizon and you're able to put in the effort to earn those opportunities.

When you're thinking negatively, take a moment to assess how realistic your thoughts truly are. Reframing your exaggeratedly negative thoughts into more realistic statements can help you maintain a healthy dose of optimism.

Bestow Positivity on Others.
While it's not your job to make everyone happy, it doesn't hurt to perk up someone's day. Once a day, share positive feedback with someone.

At work, compliment someone about a good question raised in an email or salient points that they brought up in an important meeting.

At home, praise your child for how hard they worked on their math homework. Or, tell your partner how much you appreciate them.

Making other people feel positive has lasting effects on your own life. With that, don't forget to bestow positivity on yourself.

Before bed, think about what you did during the day. Even if it was a generally lackluster day, there's bound to be something you can praise yourself for, whether it was keeping your cool when a driver cut you off or wrapping up a project that has really been a challenge for you.

Imagine a Positive Future.

It sounds kitschy, but writing down your ideas of an optimistic future can truly make a difference when it comes to your overall outlook.

If you need a primer, here's what to do: Spend 20 minutes on four consecutive days on writing down what you want to happen tomorrow, next week, next month and next year—feel free to dream big.

You can also consider a serious challenge you have in your life right now and think about possible positive outcomes.

Practice Gratitude.
Thinking about all the things you have to be grateful for, from warm sunshine to clean water, can give you an instant boost of optimism. You might even decide to keep a gratitude journal, in which you write down everything that makes you crack a smile during the day.

If nothing else, take a moment to stop, smile and be grateful for the good things in your life. Savor the moments that make it possible for you to have a good life.
It's hard to be optimistic without feeling gratitude toward those that helped you get to that happy place.

While thinking about how grateful you are is helpful, sharing your gratitude with others provides added benefits. You'll spread a bit of joy and cheer when you tell others how much you appreciate them.

Write a letter to someone who made a positive impact on your life, whether it's a teacher, a former boss or even your mom. If possible, deliver that letter in person.

Bottom Line Stay Positive....

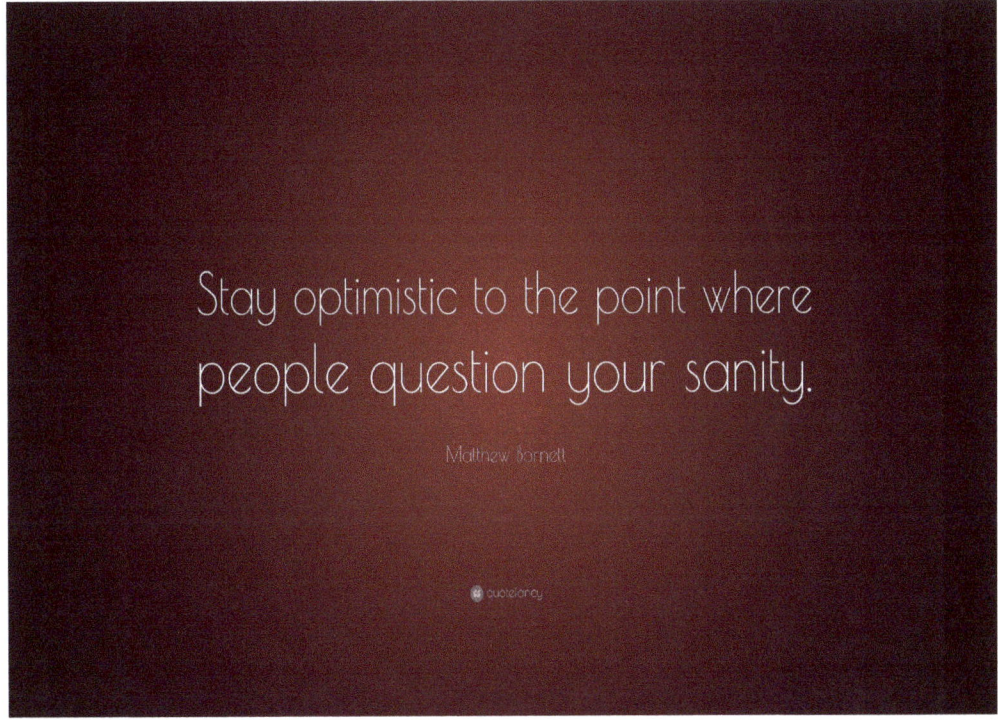

CHAPTER THREE

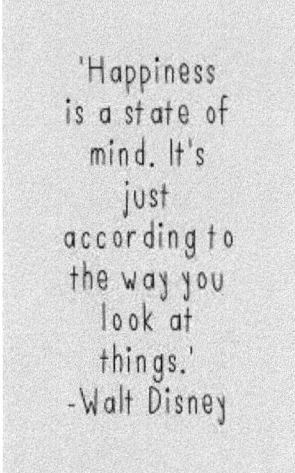

THE HAPPY STATE

There is a happiness set point for getting all the happiness that you want in life. Researchers have stated that this set point determines 50% of your happiness. They note that 10% of your happiness can be due to circumstances, both positive and negative (e.g. winning the lottery or discovering you have a terminal disease). This leaves 40% of your happiness that is determined by "intentional activity." It is under your control. It's in your hands. You have it in you and you can make it happen if you want to.

Being happier does not just mean that you smile and laugh all the time or that you find everything that you do to be a pleasurable activity or that you are in a good frame of mind all of the time, positive emotions are only one aspect of happiness. Being happy takes much more than that because there are many areas to happiness. The first is positive engagement.

Positive engagement occurs when you are so fully engaged in what you are doing that you lose track of time. You are mindful of and are in the "flow" with what you are engaged in and this ultimately means that you will be more productive and feel engaged. If you look inward carefully, you will find that there will only be very few things that you would engage in so captivatingly that you would lose track of time. These things, when you do them are the things that will truly make you happy.

The next aspect of happiness is having purpose and meaning. There is nothing like having a sense of purpose and belonging to a cause or community. When you believe in what you are doing and it is consistent with your values, you will feel a greater sense of fulfillment and life satisfaction. Accomplishment is a critical factor in experiencing life satisfaction. When you strive to achieve your goals and exhibit resilience or resolve to go through the tough times no matter how hard they come, you will feel more fulfilled.

In addition to this, experiencing positive relationships is another critical component to a happy disposition; having a friend at work or in a work team is bound to make you feel more relevant and more likely to engage in such an environment.

People, the world over are fascinated by the power of resilience and the ability to bounce back from hardships and live impactful lives. Think of Oprah Winfrey, why do you think her show was on television for more than twenty-two years? It was because people love listening to how others overcome challenges, and triumph over hardships. Think of a person that you admire greatly. It may be someone from your workplace, from your community or even a historical figure. The most likely reason you admire them may be that they have a compelling personal story about meeting a challenge, getting to the other side and remaining happy no matter what.

One very important thing to note is that the circumstances in which you find yourself does not determine what happens to you, instead, it's how you react to your circumstances that is the most important factor in determining how you scale through such circumstances - up and away from it or down and further into it.

A group of nearly 700 people on the island of Kauai starting with infants were studied. Many of these infants were from poor families and had alcoholic or mentally ill parents who were mostly out of work as they raised these infants. It was noticed that of the children who grew up in these very troubled situations, about two-thirds exhibited problematic behaviors like alcoholism, drug and substance abuse and teenage pregnancy in their late teens.

On the other hand, one third of these teens did not display these troubling behaviors. They turned out well and didn't show any signs that they had the type of backgrounds they did. When they were interviewed and asked why they turned out that way, their response most often was that they saw what their background was like and it destroyed the lives of those who toed that path. They decided that they didn't want that part of life in their future and worked towards achieving just that.

From this study and others, it was concluded that "what we do affects how we feel just as much as how we feel affects what we do."

The following are salient points drawn out from these studies

1. Practice self-care. When you take care of your physical, emotional, and mental well-being, it makes you a healthy and happier person.

2. Do the things you love. It could be as simple as reading a book out in the park or volunteering at an old people's home.

3. If it's something that gives you joy to do or participate in, it will bring you tremendous happiness. Helping others find meaning in life has also be found to help the helper find happiness in life as well.

4. Have at least one person you care about: This person does not have to be related to you or even be a significant other. The thought of making another happy and fulfilled goes a long way to make you happy and fulfilled too. That is why humans are referred to as social beings.

5. Be around other humans to thrive and we do better when it is someone we love and care about.

Know what you want out of life and go for only that: The teens in the study above who grew to be responsible and proactive adults knew what they wanted out of life and went for it. They didn't let their circumstances dictate how they turned out. They called the shots and dictated for life. They saw the hopelessness in a drug-addicted lifestyle and chose something better and more rewarding.

CHAPTER FOUR

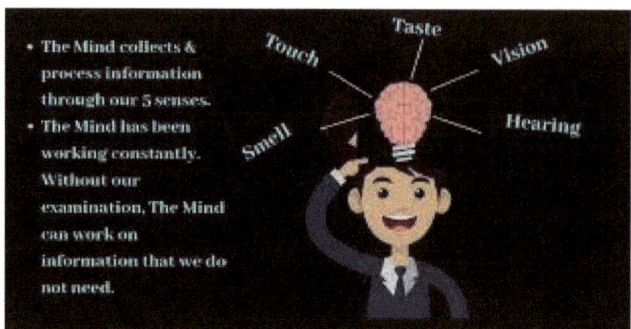

PRACTICE MIND CONTROL

When you're depressed you don't think negatively, you **believe** negatively

The first thing to ask yourself when you want to learn how to control your mind is "what exactly are you trying to change?" You need to know why you are trying to control your mind or that of other people around you. Is it to be able to focus better to be more in control of the thoughts that go on in your head. There are many types of mind control methods but the three that I use intentionally to get the results that I desire are mind exercises, creative visualization and electronic mind control.

When you practice mind exercises, you talk to your mind and tell it what you do and what you expect from it. Mind exercises help you to stay in charge of the thoughts in your head. It gives you a greater degree of self-awareness and prompts you to take action. People who are self-aware know how they feel and what they think, and are able to use that information to lead more effectively. They know how they are perceived by others and take into account how they present themselves to other people. Self-aware leaders know their strengths and their weaknesses and work to improve better in their areas of strengths.

Self-awareness is an important factor in living well and being successful. When you are aware of your emotions, strengths, weaknesses, values, and biases, you are more aware of what you are doing. You are better able to make decisions, react to adversity, and move towards realistic goals. When you are self-aware, you are open to feedback, new ideas, continuously learning and developing as a person. In relating with people in any sphere of society, self-awareness is the key to success.

Daniel Goleman identifies self-awareness as:

The fundamental emotional competence. Lacking that ability, we are vulnerable… to being sidetracked by emotions that run amok. Such awareness is our guide in fine-tuning on-the-job performance of every kind, managing our unruly feelings, keeping ourselves motivated, tuning in with accuracy to the feelings of those around us, and developing good work-related social skills, including those essential for leadership and teamwork

Self-awareness acts as that voice that we hear from within which guides our thoughts and actions. In life, we go through all kinds of situations some, good, others not so palatable and we need to respond to these events. By having self-awareness, we ensure that the way we respond to these issues reflect our own values and by doing so, we have more control over our lives. Self-awareness also serves to guide us in our interactions with others. We often experience strong emotions when we interact with others. By recognizing our own "buttons" and the things which push us, we are better able to modulate our responses when others "push" them. As we modulate our responses, we determine how people respond to us and take control of the conversation and connection every single time.

Let me explain further using this story: Many years ago, a young lady, Mary hung up the phone, feeling sad and angry. After 23 years working diligently at an insurance company, she had just received a phone call from her boss, telling her that she would not be getting the promotion that she was certain she deserved - and had earned. To add insult to injury, he also told her in the same phone call that one of her colleagues had been promoted to the higher position and she would now be reporting to her this person. As if that were not enough, she was told she would not be considered for any other higher level roles in the following year. She would have to wait till two years time. Mary remembers how she felt after receiving that phone call. "I had a couple of choices. One was to get really angry and bitter about it all, take out her frustration on anyone who happened to come along at that time and stay on at then job.

The other choice was to try to find a way out. To look for another job in a different place and into a different role and explore what might come from that. She knew that if she stayed on at the job, she would remain bitter at her boss and would find it hard to report to and work with her colleague who had been promoted to become her direct superior so she made the second choice. And in doing so, she learn a great deal about herself and what was really important in her life.

Mary's story continues: This increased self-awareness was triggered by something that was going on in another part of her life. Around the time, she received that call from her boss, Mary learned that a very close friend of hers had been diagnosed with terminal breast cancer. This difficult event that her friend had to deal with helped Mary to go deep within herself to determine what was really important in her own life at that point.

It seemed like everything bad happened all at once and it helped to put things into perspective for her. It's work. She decided that it was not a matter of life and death if She got the promotion or didn't get it but she knew at that time that she needed to enjoy her life as much as she could while she still had it. She could either decide to stay on a job that she knew she would be angry or bitter going to every morning or she could look for another one where she wouldn't have to see or report to the colleague-turned-boss.

Another thing that helped her get through and to make sense of it was asking herself the question: **'Why is this happening to me,** and what's this all about?" Following on this awareness of what was important to her, Mary carefully crafted her response to this adversity. She ultimately chose to explore alternatives within the company as opposed to acting like a victim and becoming bitter.

She used her self-awareness to develop a positive working relationship with her new boss. This led to another management position and ultimately, after a few other challenges, to a role in which she is widely valued. She has become a respected leader within her company, serving as an informal mentor to colleagues in need.

She says, "one thing she found helpful, is when she see other people she care about go through something like this. Since it happened to her, She made an attempt to reach out and help them as much as she can through the transition she went through - the emotional side of it."

So for Mary, it was the terrible news at work and in her personal life that led to an exploration of what was really important for her. Her increased self-awareness led her to a place of increased positivity and possibility. You can get in the pity party and be angry and bitter and mad about not getting the promotion that you know you deserve and put your physical and emotional health at risk or you can choose to do right by yourself and do things differently. I realized when my friend passed, that life is not a dress rehearsal and I told myself that I was going to make the best of these times and move on. It's akin to kind of always building a new house when the other one caves in on you. Staying stuck doesn't seem like a choice to me."

Being self-aware helps you take charge of your life and be in control of your mind. It helps you see things in ways that are self-empowering. When you are aware of the things you like or the way you will react to issues, it helps you to face such issues proactively. There will be no guess work because you have a good understanding of what you want and you will be able to convey that to the people you have to deal with.

You should know however that our logical minds are not our only source of information, we also get information from our feelings and intuition. The feelings we feel come from within us but they are expressed physically. We hold our emotions in our bodies, and that's why you are checking in with your physical self to see what information your body has for you. Sometimes when you make a decision based on logic, but it doesn't feel right, those feelings affect the implementation of that decision and undermine what you were trying to achieve in the first place.

When you have a decision to make, don't just rely on your mind, check in with your gut as well. Take a moment to relax into your chair. Scan your body and ask yourself about the decision you are making. What feelings are you experiencing? Are they positive or negative? Does your intuition or "gut sense" have anything to tell you? I don't have to tell you that if you do not feel good about doing something, then probably you shouldn't do it.

To develop self-awareness, determine what thought or behavior you want to become more aware of, then watch yourself over the next week. For example, if you want to become a leader who collaborates more with other people in a team, watch when you choose to not work with others. What stopped you from making a request or including them? The reasons you discover of yourself will help you work better at cooperating with others.

In the same vein, notice when you take actions that are more collaborative than your normal behavior. What helped you take the risk of changing your behavior? How did others react to you? Were their reactions surprising and positive or were they indifferent and negative? What were the benefits of your actions?

These observations of that you make of yourself are what I mean by self-awareness. You increase your internal conversations and awareness before you take action. Your actions are bigger, better, and more intentional based on this increased understanding of self.

To enjoy good health, to bring true happiness to one's family, to bring peace to all, one must first discipline and control one's own mind.-Budda

Become the CEO of Your Own Brain in Six Easy Steps. Melanie Greenberg Ph.D. The Mindful Self-Express

STEP 1: LISTEN AND ACKNOWLEDGE

Like all good leaders, you're going to have to listen to your disgruntled employee, and acknowledge that you're taking its message seriously. Minds, like people, can relax and let go when they feel heard and understood. Practice gratitude and thank your mind for its contribution. "Thank you, mind, for reminding me that if I don't succeed in making more sales, I might get fired." "Thank you for telling me that I may always be alone and never find love and have a family." "These are important areas of life, and I need to pay attention to them, and do my best to take advantage of every opportunity that comes up. I also need to learn from past experiences so I don't keep making the same mistakes."

STEP 2: MAKE PEACE WITH YOUR MIND

You may not like what your mind does or the way it conducts itself. In fact, all that negativity can be downright irritating sometimes. But the fact is, you're stuck with it and you can't (or wouldn't want to) just lobotomize it away. In the Book, *The Happiness Trap,* Dr Russ Harris uses the example of the Israelis and the Palestinians to illustrate your relationship with your mind's negative thoughts. These two old enemies may not like each other's way of life, but they're stuck with each other. If they wage war on each other, the other side retaliates, and more people get hurt and buildings destroyed. Now they have a whole lot less energy to focus on building the health and happiness of their societies. Just as living in peace would allow these nations to build healthier and more prosperous societies, so making peace with your mind – accepting that negative thoughts and feelings will be there -that you can't control them, can allow you to focus on your actions in the present moment, so you can move ahead with your most important goals without getting all fouled up.

You don't necessarily have to like the thoughts or agree with them – you just have to let them be there in the background of your mind, while you go out and get things done.

STEP 3: REALIZE YOUR THOUGHTS ARE JUST THOUGHTS

Most of the time we don't "see" our minds. They just feel like part of us! Dr Steve Hayes, the founder of Acceptance and Commitment Therapy, uses the concept of being "Fused with your thoughts" to illustrate this relationship. To be fused means to be stuck together, undifferentiated. You feel like your thoughts and feelings are YOU and so you accept them unconditionally as the truth without really looking at them. "I'm thinking I'm a failure and boring – gee, I must be a failure and boring. Well. Isn't that nice? Now I feel really wonderful." This kind of simplistic logic seems to prevail because we can't see our own minds, so we have difficulty stepping outside ourselves and getting an objective observer's perspective.

In actuality, our thoughts are passing, mental events, influenced by our moods, states of hunger or tiredness, physical health, hormones, sex, the weather, what we watched on TV last night, what we ate for dinner, what we learned as kids, and so on. They are like mental habits. And, like any habits, they can be healthy or unhealthy, but they take time to change. Just like a couch potato can't get up and run a marathon right away, we can't magically turn off our spinning negative thought/feeling cycles without repeated practice and considerable effort. And even then, our overactive amygdalas will still send us the negative stuff sometimes.

STEP 4: OBSERVE YOUR OWN MIND

The saying "Know thine enemy." is also applicable to our relationship with our own minds. Just like a good leader spends his time walking through the offices, getting to know the employees, so we need to devote time to getting to know how our minds work day to day. Call it mindfulness, meditation, or quiet time. Time spent observing your mind is as important as time spent exercising. When you try to focus your mind on the in and out rhythm of your breath, or on the trees and flowers when you walk in nature, what does your mind do? If it's like mine, it wanders all over the place – mostly bringing up old worries or unsolved problems from the day. And, if left unchecked, it can take you out of the peacefulness of the present moment, and into a spiral of worry, fear, and judgment.

Mindfulness involves not only noticing where your mind goes when it wanders, but also gently bringing it back to the focus on breath, eating, walking, loving, or working. When you do this repeatedly over months or years, you begin to retrain your runaway amygdala. Like a good CEO, you begin to know when your mind is checked out or spinning its wheels, and you can gently guide it to get back with the program. When it tries to take off on its own, you can gently remind it that's it's an interdependent and essential part of the whole enterprise of YOU.

STEP 5: RETRAIN YOUR MIND TO REWIRE YOUR BRAIN

There is an old and rather wise saying, "We are what we repeatedly do." To this, I would add "We become what we repeatedly think." Over long periods, our patterns of thinking become etched into the billions of neurons in our brains, connecting them together in unique, entrenched patterns. When certain brain pathways – connections between different components or ideas – are frequently repeated, the neurons begin to "fire" or transmit information together in a rapid, interconnected sequence. Once the first thought starts, the whole sequence gets activated.

Autopilot is great for driving a car, but no so great for emotional functioning. For example, you may have deep-seated fears of getting close to people because you were mistreated as a child. To learn to love, you need to become aware of the whole negative sequence and how it's biasing your perceptions, label these reactions as belonging to the past, and refocus your mind on present-moment experience. Over time, you can begin to change the wiring of your brain so your prefrontal cortex (the executive center, responsible for setting goals, planning and executing them), is more able to influence and shut off your rapidly firing, fear-based amygdala (emotion control center). And, this is exactly what brain imaging studies on effects of mindfulness therapy have shown.

STEP 6: PRACTICE SELF-COMPASSION

The pioneer of Self-Compassion research, Dr Kristin Neff, described this concept as "A healthier way of relating to yourself." And that's exactly what it is. While we can't easily change the gut-level feelings and reactions that our minds and bodies produce, we can change how we respond to these feelings. Most of us were taught that vulnerabile feelings, are signs of weakness – to be hidden from others at all costs. Or "Let Sleeping Dogs Lie." These bits of common-sense philosophy were dead wrong! Authors,such as Dr. Brene Brown, provide us with a convincing, research-based argument that expressing your vulnerability can be a source of strength and confidence, if properly managed.

When we judge our feelings —we lose touch with the benefits of those feelings. They are valuable sources of information about our reactions to events in our lives, and they can tell us what is most meaningful and important to us. Emotions are signals telling us to reach out to for comfort or to take time out to rest and replenish ourselves. Rather than criticizing ourselves, we can learn new ways of supporting ourselves in our suffering. We may deliberately seek out inner and outer experiences that bring us joy or comfort – memories of happy times with people we love, the beauty of nature, creative self-expression. Connecting with these resources can help us navigate the difficult feelings while staying grounded in the present.

SUMMARY

To be a successful CEO of your own mind, you need to listen, get to know your employee, acknowledge its contribution, realize it's nature, make peace with it, implement a retraining or employee development program, and treat it kindly. It will repay you with a lifetime of loyalty and service to the values and goals that you most cherish.

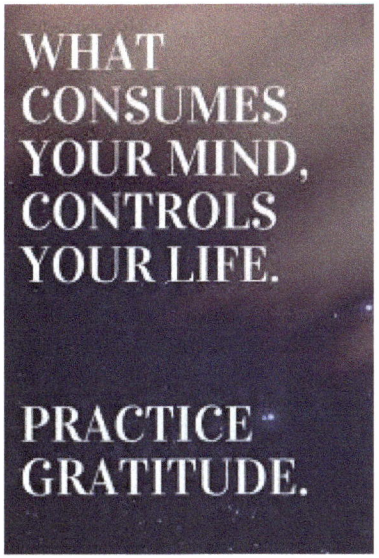

Control the WAR

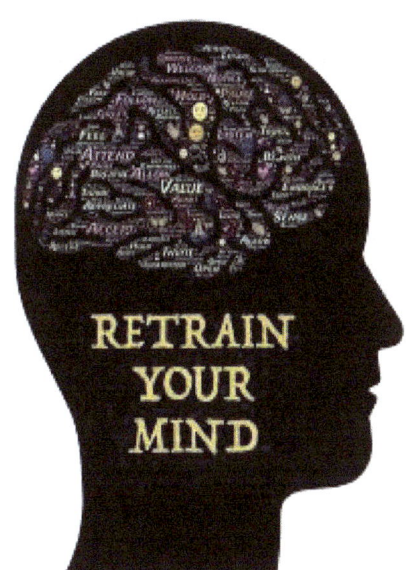

CHAPTER FIVE

THE POWER OF REFLECTION

Think about a specific event in your work or life that you would like to dwell upon and explore. Take the time to review the following questions as they apply to that specific situation.

The questions make up the Reflection Framework and it is a tool to help uncover the beliefs and values that influence your thoughts and feelings and which in turn, guide or drive your actions. Reflection is a powerful tool you can use to evaluate and gauge your own actions in relation with what you could have actually done. The reflection questions you can use in any situation include the following.

1. How did you assess what the likely outcome of your actions will be before you acted on them?

2. What other alternatives did you consider before you acted?

3. What risk factors did you weigh before you acted?

4. How accurate were your assessments of risks and outcomes that occurred?

5. To what extent did the actual outcomes match your intentions?

6. What unanticipated outcomes occurred as a result of your action?

The following sets of questions are in relation to the behavior you put up when the event occurred.

1. What were you doing? (Remember that speaking is an action!)

2. How did your behavior contribute to the consequences?

3. To what extent did you plan your actions?

4. To what extent did the actual behaviors you exhibited match the plan?

5. To what extent did your actions match your intentions?

Now, in relation to your thoughts, the following reflection questions are vital

1. What were you thinking at the moment you acted?

2. What "private messages" were you sending to yourself?

3. Did you privately test the validity of your thinking?

4. Did you privately test the validity of your thinking putting others into consideration in the situation?

In terms of how you felt in the situation

1. How were you feeling?

2. How did you become aware of those feelings?

3. What were the physical or emotional cues?

4. How did you express these feelings?

5. Did you "mask" your emotions (i.e express another emotion other than what you were actually feeling)?

6. What did you do to "take care of any emotions you were feeling at the time?

Concerning values, the following reflection questions are important:

1. Which of your espoused values were relevant to the situation?

2. Given what you did, what would you say was most important to you at the time?

3. What were you really caring about?

4. In other words, what operational values actually informed your actions?

5. What kinds of actions would have been more consistent with your espoused values?

In your anticipation of the future, the following questions are vital:

1. What were you hoping for?

2. What was your wildest dream for a productive interaction?

3. What were you afraid might happen?

4. How did the outcomes compare with what you anticipated?

5. How might changing your hopes or fears have affected other elements of the framework?

How does your past impact on the way you reflect on what you do:

1. What memories did the situation bring up for you?

2. How did memories from your past influence your thinking/private messages? Your values? Your emotions? Your actions?

In terms of organizational context, the following questions are important:

1. What aspects of the organizational culture influenced you in this situation?

2. Were your actions and thinking consistent with the organizational context?

3. Was the organizational context consistent with your personal values?

4. In what ways were you consciously supporting or opposing the organizational context?

As a social being that you are, the following questions will help determine how your actions affect others:

1. What aspects of the social culture influenced you in this situation?

2. What power dynamics were at play in the situation?

3. How were you benefiting from unearned privilege?

   4. How were you feeling the negative effects of the privilege of others?

   5. How did the context and power dynamics influence other elements of the framework (thinking, feeling, values, etc.)?

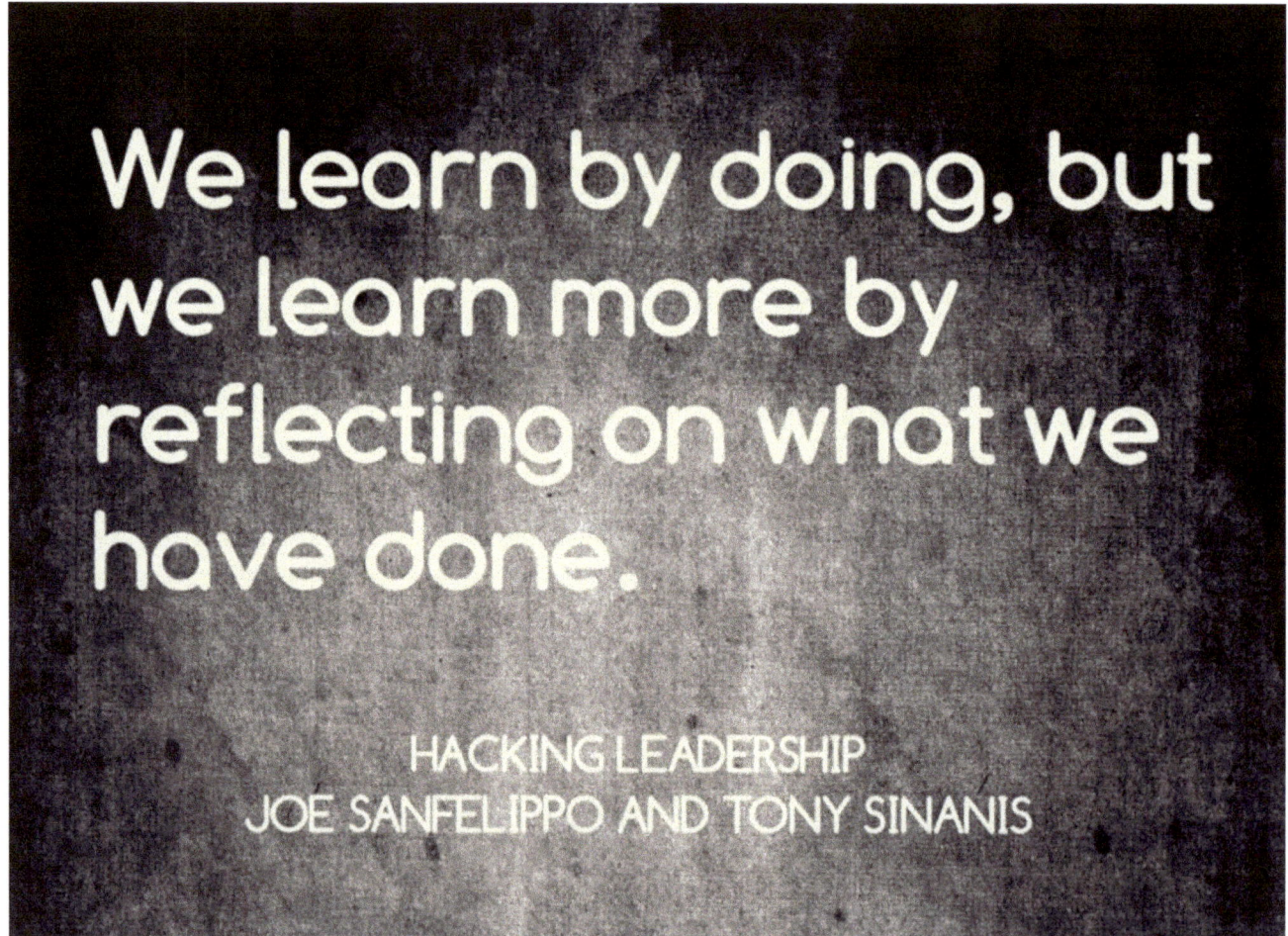

CHAPTER SIX

SECRETS AND SURPRISES

A **secret** is any information that a person intends to conceal from one or more other people.

You must have been told that it's always best to live your life like an open book. People say that it's best not to have secrets because it will show you forth as a transparent person. People believe that some of the qualities of a good person are openness and transparency. However, this doesn't apply in all cases. While there may be things that you will reveal to close family members about your life, there are also things that are certain things that you should keep private to yourself.

This is because, telling others about them will achieve nothing and if peradventure your enemies get to find about it, more, it will cause more harm than good. So, the smart thing is to not to tell anyone about it. Research has shown that keeping secrets weigh down on the person keeping it even when there is little danger of the secret been uncovered. It has also been found that people who keep secrets are often distracted by thoughts of their secrets thus they may find seemingly simple tasks overwhelming. They may find that the journey to a particular destination takes longer than it should or may find performing task more difficult than it should be.

However, that is not to say that keeping secrets is altogether bad. There are times and situations where it is absolutely necessary to keep things secret to yourself.

When you keep your goals to yourself, you give yourself permission to **succeed.** This is because when you talk about your goals, it conditions your mind into thinking that it has succeeded when in actual fact it has done no such thing. This false sense of effort diminishes the likelihood that you will actually take the step that carry out your goal.

The element of surprise sometimes comes into play and it happens when you do things that you would ordinarily not do. But why is it important to surprise people? Surprise works on the system of dopamine in the brain and helps to focus your attention or create new path ways of better responses and relationship.

It is the psychological and emotional response to experiences that you give that does not align with another person's paradigm and expectations.

Psychologically, surprise appeals to you and I. It makes is tick. It keeps us excitable. The human brain is wired in such a way that it turns its attention to things that are new or changing. That's why you will always check your Whatsapp and Facebook messenger for unread messages. You want to read or know about the next big thing. Your brain likes the dopamine drip that takes place every time you check for and receive a new message.

Now, after all has been said and done? There is a flip side to the coin. Boredom happens when the brain lacks stimulation. It's craving that dopamine — the dash of unexpected, the dosage of challenge, the difference of setting, the need for curiosity, and the interruption of patterns. Surprise can overcome customer's reluctance, and make them buy from you. This is because surprise creates an emotional fluctuation in a person's experience, they become more likely to do (or not to do) certain things.

When some people get angry or they are hurt, they do things that they know they shouldn't do. When others become grief-stricken, they act in ways that go against common sense. In the same vein, when people get surprised, they respond in a way that may different from how they would normally respond, based on life paradigms.

In other words, if you can effectively and positively surprise someone, you can influence them. How you influence them depends on how you surprise them.

So in conclustion: Live your life like a **PIMP, PLAYER & MURDERER....**

Do not go yet; One last thing to do
If you enjoyed this book or found it useful I'd be very grateful if you'd post a short review on Amazon. Your support really does make a difference and I read all the reviews personally so I can get your feedback and make this book even better.

Thanks again for your support!

www.ingramcontent.com/pod-product-compliance
Lightning Source LLC
Chambersburg PA
CBHW040752020526
44118CB00042B/2922